About the Author

First published collection, *Quintessence*, Brandywine Books, Burns, TN. 1992, several individual pieces published in local magazines, newspapers and anthologies including *Oyez Review*, Roosevelt University, Chicago, IL. The author has worked with local school with the fourth grade class, culminating in a collection of every child's poem. He has worked with area artists in the impression of his poems through music and visual art. Mike has performed in several coffeehouses in the past both reading his work and doing improv poetry.

This collection is dedicated to Roslyn, my sounding board and mate. It is also a tribute to all who have helped shape my life through the years. Hope you enjoy the contents.

Michael John Carignan

CHRYSALIS

AUSTIN MACAULEY PUBLISHERS™

LONDON • CAMBRIDGE • NEW YORK • SHARJAH

Ordering Information
Quantity sales: Special discounts are available on quantity purchases by corporations, associations, and others. For details, contact the publisher at the address below.

Publisher's Cataloging-in-Publication data
Carignan, Michael John
Chrysalis

ISBN 9781649793652 (Paperback)
ISBN 9781649794185 (Hardback)
ISBN 9781649794192 (ePub e-book)

Library of Congress Control Number: 2021914280

www.austinmacauley.com/us

First Published 2021
Austin Macauley Publishers LLC
40 Wall Street, 33rd Floor, Suite 3302
New York, NY 10005
USA

mail-usa@austinmacauley.com
+1 (646) 5125767

I would like to thank my girlfriend, family, and friends for their support in this endeavor.

Wet haven solace from

                  the heavens of the sky

     trailing circular puddles

                mirroring daily memories

                    as others burrow deep

                  in the catacombs of

                          the soul

              relationships tender

                  teeter on the balconies

                    on the outcome

                    of the past

                      and   what   may

            become

                    the birth of

                        today.

Cloud of nocturnal visions
    drift in my slumber
        a bear like canine
            lifting me up in tenderness-
                an apartment of experiences
                set in the past like
                    old mismatched chairs
                        waiting   for   the
                dust to
                            settle
                as I sit down to
                    try and figure out
                    the   meaning
                behind
                    the realm
        maybe skeletons
                embalmed in repression
                    struggle to smell
                freedom's air.

It is like the sparrow
and the dove
fluttering about as my heart
does for you
the lady draped in
a gown of loving worlds
of histories of
compassion that
coming home to her
is a foundation of
stability that is
so hard to find
in a garden of weeds
she is but the flower
unveiling her blossoms
to the welcoming sun

tribute to roz-.

The reassurance

of my love cradled next

to me in sleep

the hollow impressions

in my pillow as

the night unfolds

and visions pranced

about

in their rem game

consciousness darts up

now and again

to test the waters of

reality

you are there

covering the

blankets

over my

bare shoulders

comforting me

like

a tired

soldier arriving

from the wars of

the day

my love is like

a tapestry

sculptured a

prism

of emotion

arms embracing you

tears savored

in an
invisible tea cup
till eternity.

Almond-back conch
        back to the sun
            mouth whispering
                to a population of pebbles
                    the secrets of the world
                    on a beach washed up
                            with sand dollars
                                with their own
                price
                            to pay
                an innocent child
                        picks one up
                            playing with it
                in
                            his hands
                        a relic of time
                        before him.

The dragon breathes
        insufferable paradoxes of fire
                extinguishing anything in his wake
                until he realizes that the
                        man who can't find
                        his shoes can't
                            run away from
                              the reality that
                            slumber
                      only hint at
                        only
                    partake in
                the final outcome
                a clown without his
                    grease paint with
              the curtain going up
                as a new crowd gathers
                    to judge the show.

Chrysalis
throbbing beauty
breaking out of
of her wispy gown
wet wings testing
the open air
soaring high above
dark thunderous clouds
to the uninhibited realm
seemingly without
a single care
landing on
a throne of flowers
a tiny flutter
in her own
utopia.

White dough gingerly lay down
          to the whining of metal monsters
               plummeting into molds driven
                    to the inferno of the oven
                         after Hansel and Gretel
                              throw in the witch
                         as workers bent
                              in stress attempt
                         to corral the hordes
                              shooting down the
          line
               like some kind
                    of cattle round-up
               as whole populations
                    of buns die
                         upon the floor
               while the successful ones
                    shipped out in
               busy trucks to
               be consumed by
                    hungry people on
                    a lazy summer day.

Master edition
a collector's prize
a trophy gleaming
untarnished by the
onslaught of age
the virtues every one
possesses deep inside
holding strong against
others who challenge
to charge through
the barricade like
the Trojan horse
to find the
soft spot of
compromise
to make us yield
our values for
acceptance
to a whole population
of a mind blind mass
serving their rituals
on a charred cold fire
like deity scouts lost on the trail.

You were once the eagle –
        majestic, strong and true –
            now entangled in
                the muck and mire of
                    your mind held hostage
                    in a struggle to be
                            set free from
                    repression and depression
                        to rise once again
            against the flaming sun
                    to rekindle your volumes
        of charm, love of others
                    love of self
        to soar above the
                dark clouds
            and into the beaming
                    proud light
        with family and friends holding
                the way for you
                    to be there
            a candle in
                a dark room dissolving
                the shadows away

tribute to Dustin.

Time sometimes
gently nudges me ahead
otherwise
contributing aches and pains
wrapping up
days gone by
visionary presents
for me to unwrap
any time
a vulnerable specter
of one
wrestling with the
game of fate.

Light angelic flakes
brush the ground as
if a white painting was
being created for
all to see
rosy red sunsets still
saturate the palette
complimenting visions
grown strong
memories like playful children
prance around the mind
building a solid foundation
for formulating what
could be the
next dream opening
the door to reality
like a tired traveler
come in from the
frigid cold for
a hot java
and a conversation
or two.

Warm fuzzy morning
            you cooking breakfast sandwiches
            idly sipping coffee with
                        Fox News
            wobbling over to you
                        for a morning kiss
            so warm inside for
                        my heart to
                        the Arctic blasts
                        outside where
                                    Jack Frost is
            celebrating a ticker tape
                        parade for
            his cold demise
                        outside
            even snow angels
                        would have their
                        halos shattered
            in the frozen realm
                        bestowed the
                        crown of reality
                        today.

Oh Roslyn,
        named after
            America's pin-up girl,
                you are an angel
                    dew drop wings
                        brushing against
                            my heart
                our journeys
                    intertwined like
                        praying hands
                        dreams pretending
                            to be phantoms
                                dancing in time
                oh Roslyn
                    with those ravishing eyes
                        prying into the pathways
                            of my soul
                oh Roslyn
                        your troubadour
                            kneels with love
                                upon your court
                    your sweet voice
                        travels the corridors
                            of my mind
                        plunging into my
                            todays and tomorrows
                                like a compassionate
                                explorer of our love
                        my white flag

waves free and proud
surrendering to every
moment with you.

Jesters in purple robes
　　　　slung bags over
　　　　　　their clown Santa Claus
　　　　　　　　backs
　　　　performing their stuff
　　　　　　in the king's court
　　　　his highness cloaked
　　　　　　in his hedonistic whims
　　　　rallies the common man
　　　　　to folly
　　　　　　so a man struggling
　　　　　　　　to be a god
　　　　　　　can soar even
　　　　　　　　　higher
　　　　　an eagle
　　　　　　caught in
　　　　　　　the strong limbs
　　　　　　　　of a solid tree.

Recounting the spring air
the sky cradled in
lemon-colored light
footsteps downtown
taking in the blur
of people with
their own missions
to take
mortality is
like a coffee cup
caffeine swimmers
swirling in a maze
until the last gulp
has settled as
the flutter of
a single heart beat
plays in a hollow drum.

Gray gossamer hallways
      escape me
        skeletons of
            the past
    claw repeatedly
       on the closet door-like Pandora's box
            a Rubik's Cube-
              confused in
                  its paradox of color
             ripples tear apart
              from the rising phoenix
             preening her labored wings
              lifting like a helicopter
               whirling from the flames
           history marching with
             a proud smile
               to be the audience
                 of tomorrow.

Aging
the willow wisp of
gray hair blowing
free from the dandelion
on a mid-summer's breeze
the little boy armed with
bamboo pole searching
for new moments to
pop their heads out
like fish teasing
the lures
each year past
as if they were but
onion skins layered
from the last
peering in the mirror
trying to find
the young child
lost in the rumble
of the man slowly
filing memories away
in a file cabinet
marked important
take out when needed
do not disturb otherwise.

Wet haven solace from

           the havens of the sky

     trailing circular puddles

             mirroring daily memories

               as others burrow deep

                in the catacombs of

                   the soul

            relationships tender

             teeter on the balconies

               on the outcome

           of the past

             and   what   may

           become

              the birth of

               today.

The sky chalkboard gray
surges into in hordes
of wispy wanderers
shedding their tears
on the thirsty ground
a mouse peeks
cautiously
of a basement floor
if the onslaught
of wet has passed
birds in their concert
of chirps heralding
in the beaming sun
brandishing a smile
on a child's face
as the innocence
of the day
has just barely
begun.

A rumpled

        unmade bed

      it is pulled together

             from me

     after you have gone

        each line smoothed out

             with love from

              your tapestry

           of dreams from

             the night before

       light beckoning

        through the window

        of more visions

         yet to march anew

       like excited children

        on Halloween

     with their candy baskets

           held high.

A murder of crows
              preening black wings
                    to a blind moon
          distant figures introduced
            in an unconscious scene
           deceased father and sister
                          guardians looking
                            down on the edge
                                of heaven's cloud
          a cup of coffee
                        burping in caffeine fits
                           to the morning's gleam
            a puzzle of mind
                    gaining momentum
                    like a roller coaster
                              gone mad
              from the thrashing
                          of the eve
                pillow imprinted
                        like an ancient fossil
              only a dream
                      striding through
                          the haze to me.

The membrane of
   a vision engulfs the
      network of a picture
        of the mind
  like lightning flashing
      in stories unfolded
    being the observer
       of a car ride through
       a circus
     fetching back clothes
        under a stage
     little children
      laughing in the background
    then waking up
      to the strong light
        of morning
   trying to discover
    like a wise man
      the meaning behind
     every boulder
      of the realm
        of mine
     new photos
      in a yellowed scrapbook.

The ripples of a
blank sky signature
the oncoming freight train
of things to come
as the little boy
of yesteryear,
with bent bamboo pole
dipped into the
watery furrows of
the Merrimack River,
still lives deep inside
ready to pounce
into tomorrows
like the old man-
of the mt-
now praying on
his stony knees
for a new vision
like a red blush
baby crying
into a new world
of what could
be.

Remember
cherry blossoms erupting in
full bloom in Japan
Buddha's smiling
in mammoth statues
unveiling like a hidden prize
years later – of the love
you transcended to
your boys
sacrifices you gave
for them
you are the unsung hero
your compassion for me
and others
trickles down in streams
to gush down in
torrents that even
Noah's ark would have
trouble staying
afloat
you are the dove
holding the olive
leaf spring in
a world of chaos in,
thank you.

Mesmerizing chlorophyll martyrs
unleashing rainbow tints
sizzling bright in
herding all the shades of dark
of the land in
a hushed corner
strapped upon
boughs
swinging crazily
to the heavens
snapping free
hurdling to the ground
burning
burning brown
into autumn's memory.

The lithe wind sway
    like a dancer's nimble step
        autographing the floor
            collecting past visions
                as if they were stamps
                    pasted into a book
                        to be opened/caressed
                  in the mind's eye
                when storm clouds
              gather like
              wild dogs
            ready to devour
            any scrap of reality
          a slight smile
              a lingering touch
      turns the dark
              of a monument
                of nightmares
              into a sea of light
                for a little boy
            to discover the
              lucky sand dollar
          for the moment
    as the tide rolls back
      her cobalt hair for now.

Tormented by rivers
of indifference from
how change has to
disguise me in
a new suit
receipts lost – no return
I paint my best smile
pushing down the hordes
of feelings best
not played out
like a bad hand of poker
dead man's hand
last weathered
cowboy hat
garnishing a table
crowded by
spectators of
the paradise
of the charts
cobwebs
marooning the past.

The glimmer of
    the swirls of the
        Merrimack River
           on a summer youth's day
              a brown-haired boy casting bamboo pole
           down into a pool
                    of dreams yet
         unfolded like
          an oriental fan
           an origami napkin
             evolving into so
                    many shapes
           the old man of
                the mountain
            now praying on
             his stony knees
      years try to blur
            ancient memories
              but like King Tut's tomb
             no matter how
         deep they are buried
         they are always
               rediscovered.

As the monarchs unfurl
        their silk gowns
    with weathered leaves
        drooping down from
           naked boughs
      you are my light
         in a sea of darkness
           I can whisper my
             thoughts in a den
                 of fools
        but your voice
          is the only one
          that makes a difference
                 to me
          as the wind
            tickles the clouds
              with crystal bandits
                soon to fall.

Thought healthy genes
ran a marathon through me
until the hordes of chills
and body racking coughs
took over
an ambulance ride
in a snowstorm
into a sterile playground
of needles and IVs
brought one back
to the living
magnified by the
care and love
of a girlfriend
that no thanks is
enough of
a gratitude stenciled
in every thought of her
a busy bee empowered
by his queen
in a hive of
visions yet
to be.

As a kid working
        at Rexall's drug store
            for Mr. Griffith
                donned in white
                    starched smock
                        instructing a young boy
                upstairs to find
                            some item
                instead exposed
                        to a maze of rooms
                    an old forgotten ballroom
                        dust from the
                            speakeasies
                phantoms circling in
                            dance from
                    an era
                        lost in time.

Sparse down winter
   crystal mounds weeping
      to their own demise
  loved ones fading
     into a land of colors
       of angels carrying them
     to a realm that is
      beyond our understanding
      our tears left
        on the town line
         of heaven
       our love in
        a package bound
        in mortality
       that we were left
       behind to understand
        it all
      a dusty book
       in a forgotten aisle
       in a library
         yet unread.

The starkness of the shadows
gripping the winter sidewalks
looming like mysterious phantoms
of days waning through
time's door
always startled me as if
it was an omen to
gather up all the
pleasant memories
in a basket marked self
with the assumption to
add more
always more
while today weaves
the fabric of
tomorrow.

Proud eagle with-
    snow-colored head
        stencils the rainbow sky
           with each swoop of
                his airplane wings
                  swooping down talons
                      to catch his prey
                hopefully we can
                  be like this mighty bird
                    facing our mistakes
                  like the lost mouse
                building a tower
                  of better things to be.

Pools of stained crystal angels
mourn the hungry pavements
homeless don their cardboard signs
in hopes for a hand-out
life pitches sometimes bitter turns
accented against better times
a loved sister in her favorite chair
surrounded by her
loyal canines
nothing seems fair
memories collected in
a cerebral basket with
a fragile sticker pasted
all over
a sister left behind
to gather the pieces
who is loved by
a man who wants
to help her in
any way he can.

Sneakers swung over
telephone poles while
screeching of vagrant crows
mask the horizon with
initials of black
a vision within
the catacomb of slumber
wakes consciousness to
carefully place the pieces
of the puzzle together
examining close to
see if a whole picture
has formed like
a goddess dedicated
to prose.

Hickory dickory dock
the mouse ran up the clock
time stood still
much to mother goose's thrill
as spoon full of sunshine
found slumber's ground
painting the darkness
with hopes and visions
while Humpty Dumpty
put them all back
together again
in days to come
of pleasantness and fun
of a huge parade
of smiles as the
rolling clouds
engulf the smiles
of tomorrows
hickory dickory dock.

Freshly mowed grass
    sitting on the front porch
     with my father
       guessing where each driver's lives
were like climbing up and down
    willow hill
               a sister dressing up
          like a nun teaching class
            on Saturday mornings in the cellar
            the days of wearing
             innocence like a hat
              in a movie that
               had just found
                the beginning of
              a story with a screenplay
               that was still being
                written.

Laughter spiraling down
　　on the beaten leaves
　　　splashing their receding colors
　　　　on the November ground
　　　　a neighborhood bus stop
　　　　kidnapped by
　　　　　sex, drugs, and drunks
　　　waiting for a destination
　　　　　never to be
　　　　　　for most except
　　those willing to search
　　　for the rainbow after
　　　　the onslaught of the
　　　　rain.

Strangled holidays in
the mind
nocturnal bliss curled up
like a Cheshire cat not
conscious where his
food bowl slinked off to
like the mad hatter took it
in the veiled version
of reality when
the curtains are pulled down
after a full day of thought
then slumber rolls in
like high tide
the very fibers of your being
expanding the boundaries
of the imagination that
you had cornered in
the cerebral prison
where the warden
is who is peering back
in the reflection of a mirror
of a colossal dream
in a realm of maybes.

9 781649 793652